My Grandmother Has a Chandelier!

My Grandmother Has a Chandelier!

JEANNETTE KEARNS

Illustrated by Mel Holzsager

VANTAGE PRESS
New York

Published by Vantage Press, Inc.
516 West 34th Street, New York, New York 10001

Manufactured in the United States of America
ISBN: 0-533-12064-0

Library of Congress Card No.: 96-90470

0 9 8 7 6 5 4 3 2 1

TO MY DEAR FAMILY

Dr. John R., Kathryn, John M. & Jacqueline Kearns
and to the memory of
Walter J. Kearns and Ernest D. Forziati

Contents

Foreword

Some of the choice bits in this book come from listening to conversations the children had during their play time. They usually were relaxed and chatty, though, I must add, that when children trust a teacher, they don't hold back very much at any time—as you will see.

I repeat, the secret is *listening*.

A few of these quotes may seem X-rated to the reader, but be assured, the statements were said in total innocence.

The children from the fifties, sixties, and seventies were surely as bright as the present five- and six-year-olds, but not as worldly. Whether that is good or bad is something I do not know.

All I ask is that you keep in mind that the quotes are from the age group as stated—ages five and six—though the last chapter will be devoted to a few jewels from my own family (of course!). Except for the family names, all the others have been changed.

My teaching career was at the Radburn School in Fair Lawn, New Jersey, the borough in which my family and I resided.

1
Thinking Or Not!

I wore a fur coat to school, and many children said, "My mommy has a coat like that."

After hearing this ten or twelve times, one child said, "My mommy *wishes* she had a coat like that."

*   *   *

We were "reading pictures" in our book. A man was using a wheelbarrow to cart corn to the pigs. I asked why he didn't carry the load in his arms. Joe simply said, "He doesn't have enough arms."

*   *   *

George—looking up at me while I buttoned his hat—"Mrs. Kearns, someday I'm going to get crayons and a piece of paper and draw you a picture that you can keep—I think!"

*   *   *

On September 30th we discussed the last of the month and maintained that tomorrow would be the first day of October.

When "tomorrow" came, October 1st, I asked the children what day it was.

Said one, "It is what you said yesterday that we would have tomorrow."

*   *   *

We were having a little science lesson, discussing rain, sun, rainbows, etc.

I said, "If the sun is shining right after or during a shower, and we turn our back to the sun, what do we see?"

Said Felice, "No sun."

*   *   *

Mother's Day

I was making bath salts for the children to take home for Mother's Day. In explanation, I said I would put perfume and coloring into Epsom salts. As I proceeded to put drops of perfume into one bag, one youngster leaned over to another and whispered, "I hope she knows what she's doing."

* * *

Comment heard: "My mother isn't going to take a bath on Mother's Day."

* * *

We were talking about the days of the week. I said, "If yesterday was Wednesday, what is today?"
Answer—"Tomorrow."

*   *   *

Stephanie dropped a box of small tiles on the floor. She obviously didn't feel like picking them up, so she said to one of the boys, "Do you want to play with these?" (He didn't fall for it!)

*   *   *

Good thinking for age five. Mary-Ellen, explaining to another child about grandfathers: "You see, when my daddy was little, he had a daddy, and now his daddy is my grandfather."

*   *   *

Andrew—Is it tomorrow yet?

J.K.—It's today.

Andrew—Will tomorrow be another day?

J.K.—Yes.

Andrew—O.K., because yesterday you said to bring back the note tomorrow and I didn't bring it yet. I'll bring it when it gets to be tomorrow!

* * *

Scott was crying when we were in the playground.

I said, "What happened, Scott?"

He said, "I ran into Jonathan and hurt my head."

Turning to Jon, I said, "Where were you hit, Jon?" He said, "In the head, too, but Scott's was worse. He was running faster!"

* * *

During discussion about the Pilgrims, I asked why some people in Holland build houses on legs (high water areas).

Robyn—"Because they didn't have cars and when they wanted to go someplace, they could."

(Served me right for using "legs" rather than "poles".)

* * *

Mr. Kuhn, our principal, was retiring and the children and I were discussing it.

Said one—"Is the next Mr. Kuhn going to be a girl or boy?"

* * *

Matthew brought a toy dog carved from wood. I said, "I wonder what kind of wood that is?"

Kevin said, "It looks like dogwood to me."

* * *

The upper grades in our school had been dismissed early for a faculty meeting.

I had taken my class out to the playground and a 2nd grader, my ex-pupil, went by and said, "Hello, Mrs. Kearns."

I said, "Hello, Michael."

One of my present youngsters said, "Do you know him, Mrs. Kearns?"

I said, "Yes, he used to be in my class." She said, "Oh, but you grew up faster than he did."

* * *

Pat to me—There's a question I think you should be asking, and I have the answer to it.

J.K.—What is the question?

Pat—I don't know.

*   *   *

Judi discussed her new coat with me *every day* for two months until—she got a new hat!

*   *   *

On a very warm day in late spring, I wore sandals on bare feet when we went to the playground. Said Joe, "Your feet look old."

*   *   *

Another day I wore stockings with dark heels. Said one lad, "Mrs. Kearns has dirty heels!"

*   *   *

Katy—Here are some cookies for you, Mrs. Kearns. My mother got them at the rummage sale!

*   *   *

Robert—My tooth came out because I "bended" it.
J.K.—What did the tooth fairy leave for you?
Robert—My tooth.

*   *   *

Barbara—When I grow up, I'm going to be a queen—if I can find the queen's stuff.

*   *   *

Dean—You're a nice teacher.
J.K.—Thank you. You're a nice boy.
Dean—Thank you and my eyes are brown.

*   *   *

Question to class—Do you know the nursery rhymes?
Garry—No, I didn't go to nursery school.

*   *   *

Sean—Why couldn't they put Humpty-Dumpty back together?

Tom—They didn't have any Scotch tape.

*　　*　　*

One of the little boys was showing a new book to the group.

Larry—That's a Dr. Seuss book.

J.K.—No, it just looks like one.

Larry—Oh, well, you can't win them all!

*　　*　　*

Gillian—My grandmother had to go to the doctor.

J.K.—Why?

Gillian—She tripped on her miniskirt!

*　　*　　*

We hang clothes on the line to let the dirt fall off.

*   *   *

It had snowed quite a good deal during the night, but not enough to close the schools.

Though many children were driven to school, there were many who trudged through the five or six inches of snow in time for the 8:45 AM start of classes.

Outer clothing was hung in the closet adjacent to our room, but boots were lined up in the hall, on the floor, just outside our door.

Just before the 11:15 A.M. dismissal time, the children picked out their boots and brought them into the room to put them on.

Mark said, "Mrs. Kearns, I can't find my boots." I looked out and saw a pair still sitting there, saw Mark's name sewn inside, and handed them to him.

He said, "They aren't mine. Mine had snow on them."

*   *   *

2
Words—Placed & Misplaced

Language Development

The policeman was visiting our classroom, and while he was speaking to the children, the custodian, Mr. B., passed outside and was holding a rag to clean the windows.

Officer V. asked, "Who is that?"

In one voice, the children answered, "Mr. Clean!"

*   *   *

A few days after having my hair done (almost ready for another appointment), Anne said, "You had a new hairdo. Where did it go?"

*   *   *

We were discussing smoking and that we shouldn't indulge. Danny said, "My mother and daddy broke the habit and joined the unhooked generation." (Sounded like Danny remembered a statement he heard!)

*   *   *

We had had a bad ice storm and some children wore snow pants to school.

I said, "Put your snow pants on *before* your boots."

Said one boy, "Is there such a thing as ice pants?"

*   *   *

Emery said he got a $3 check for his birthday. A few days later, he mentioned it again.

I said, "You still have your check?"

He said, "Yup. I didn't get checked out yet."

*   *   *

Reported to me by a mother:

Mother to child—"I must send an excuse for your absence."

Child—"It's not an excuse. I was *really* sick."

*   *   *

(In the days of prayers in school)
"Give us this day our daily breakfast."

*　　*　　*

J.K.—What do I mean when I say that a cow is chewing her cud?
Anne—She's getting milk from her mother.

*　　*　　*

J.K.—Does anyone know another name for "Fall"?
Joanne—No, do you?

*　　*　　*

Danny had brought a tool chest and tools for Show & Tell. Said he, "We're going to build a cat house."

* * *

What is today's date? (January 22nd)
Answer—January the twenty-tooth.

* * *

At Halloween time, I asked my class what we called a pumpkin with a face. No one knew, so I prompted them with the words, "A Jack—What?"

Said Pat—"A Jack Ass."

* * *

The student traffic guards wore white belts diagonally across the shoulder and around the waist.

Amy said, "My sister is a substitute guard—she's out there wearing her garter belt."

*　　*　　*

Larry brought in a book for Show & Tell.
J.K.—Is that a library book?
Larry—No, it's an "own" book.

*　　*　　*

Patty—We heard the *Mary Poppins* record and they sang the osis song.
J.K.—Do you mean the "Supercalifragilisticexpiali-docious" song?
Patty—Yes, that's what I said!

*　　*　　*

John—My brother Peter got sick last night and sicked up all over.

*   *   *

Michael to classmates: "Teachers aren't robots. They're personal like us."

*   *   *

Susan was being annoyed by a little boy on the way to school and evidently had tried to stop him. Said she, "I don't know how his mother controls him. I can't!"

*   *   *

During his visit to the U.S., the Pope was to offer a Mass in Yankee Stadium. Said a child, "There's going to be mess in Yankee Stadium today."

* * *

I was reading a story that contained the word "frisky." I said to the children, "What does 'frisky' mean?"
Said Brian, "Whiskey."

* * *

We have a two-piece house—
upstairs and downstairs.

* * *

I knew the 6th grades were going to Hoboken on a field trip, but Katy made the announcement: "My brother is going to Nassau with his class on Monday."

J.K.—Do you mean Hoboken?

Katy—Oh, yes. That's it.

*   *   *

Kim—I wanted to write my name, but I didn't because I mistaked the M.

*   *   *

Myrna had heard the expression "this morning" very often and thought the word was "smorning." She said to me, "Every smorning my mother brings me to school."

*   *   *

Barbara—When I went to the bathroom this morning, the toilet was stopped up.

J.K.—Did you have to get a plumber?

Barbara—No, my mother plumbed it.

* * *

I put a quantity of paste on each table, but one had a little more than the others. David said, "We have the lotest."

* * *

Robert—That's *amazing*. The weatherman said it would be mild and it's mild.

* * *

Laura—Mrs. Kearns, are we allowed to make "do-do" in school?

J.K.—Yes, of course.

Laura—Well, I was making rude noises all over the place!

* * *

Michael—I can wear my jacket on the other side, too. It's flexible.

*   *   *

Gary—It's hot and I'm expiring.

*   *   *

Linda—I left my gloves in my poat cocket.

*   *   *

Bill—Our car over-boiled this morning.

*   *   *

Working on our number booklet, we were to paste a 3 and 3 circles. Up piped a little voice, Terrance, in particular, "I lost one of my balls."

*   *   *

Cole—Mrs. K, what are you making?
J.K.—A Valentine.
C.—Is that something to drink?
(Ballantine?)

*   *   *

We had a short discussion about the work of the Red Cross organization. These are two of the results:
   1. One child, after receiving a Red Cross pin, "Does this mean I can cross the street by myself?"
   2. Tom—We belong to the Blue Cross already.

*   *   *

Some language development is not the greatest—
   1. Gordon—She stinks.
      J.K.—Please don't say that again.
      Gordon—Well, she *does* smell.

   2. Dan—Mrs. Kearns, Danny has some kind of perfume on.
      J.K.—It's probably some kind of nice hair tonic.
      Dan—Well, it stinks to me. I can't stand it.

*   *   *

You're doing better than I if you can figure this out!
1st boy—(teasing another) N-O spells "yes."
2nd boy—Oh, no. It spells "no."
3rd boy—(Michael, who *always,* he thinks, knows the answer) No, S-I-T-A-E spells "yes." Also, A-C-T-L-Y spells "racket."

*   *   *

24

Another I've never been able to figure out.
Dean—I'm going to grow up to be a bachelor.
J.K.—Do you know what that means?
Dean—No.
Zachary—I do. It means you can make meatballs.

*   *   *

My little friend Tim couldn't say the "l" sound.
Before quoting him, I wish you to know that I'm not ridiculing Tim. He just sounded so cute when he spoke.

1. Our bathroom light was losing strength. Said Tim, "Mrs. Kearns, the bathroom yight is a yitta dark."
2. He was wearing boots about three sizes too big and said, "My Mom has to yet these shrink a yitta."
3. Tim, again—I can tie my shoes. I just make two yoops, twist-em and puy-em.

*   *   *

(Just a reminder, at this point, that this is the *vocabulary* chapter.)
J.K.—What does "direction" mean?
Amy—Toward the same way.

*   *   *

We were talking about adding an "s" to make a word plural. The word we were discussing was "surprises."
Patty kept saying "surprise," not adding the final "s."
I said, "What is more than one surprise?"
She said, "Surprise, surprise, surprise."

*   *   *

May I have a drink? My mouth is all fried up.

*   *   *

We were working on a project that needed some concentration. Pat was giving us a minimum of that.

I said, "Pat, see if you can concentrate a little more tomorrow."

Pat: "But I *am* constipated."

*   *   *

Charles—I'm getting a toy for Pocahantos.

J.K.—What is Pocahantos?

Charles—You know, Pocahantos around Christmastime. I'm getting a toy.

J.K.—Do you mean Hanukkah?

Charles—Oh, yes. I'm getting a toy for Hanukkah.

*   *   *

J.K.—What holiday, in addition to Christmas, do we have in December?

Ans.—Harmonica. (Hanukkah.)

* * *

A talking doll that we had in the classroom said, "What's playing at the cinema? Let's go."

Paul—The doll said, "What's playing at the synagogue?"

* * *

A five is an upside down "stew."

* * *

I'm going to You Nork.

* * *

The Christmas tree was *loaded* with decorations that we had made in the classroom.

(In the years before they were disallowed.)

Vicky—When are we going to decorate the tree?

(That statement brought about the meaning of *decorate.*)

*   *   *

I have to eliminate (go to the bathroom).

*   *   *

I put up a leprechaun for St. Patrick's Day and asked what holiday it was for.

Answer—Passock (Passover)

*   *   *

Asked of a doctor's daughter—
"What is a stethoscope for?"
Answer—To breathe people.

*   *   *

The visiting police officer was showing handcuffs to the children and asked if anyone knew what they were called.

1st answer—cuff-hands.
2nd answer—hand cops.

*   *   *

During the pledge of allegiance:
"One nation, under guard."

* * *

J.K. to Wendy: I hope your cold doesn't get worse.
Wendy—No, it's getting gooder.

* * *

We were reviewing information about the Pilgrims and the town of Scrooby, where they had lived.
I asked the name of the town.
Robert answered—"Screwball."

* * *

Amy was talking about a ship. Karen misunderstood and said, "It's not nice to say words like that."

Said Amy, "I said 'ship,' not 'sh—!' "

*   *   *

Steven—We went fishing and I caught a "shiny" (sunny).

*   *   *

J.K.—What's another name for Fall? (Season)
Answer—Winterfall.

*   *   *

During a lesson on tree parts:
J.K.—What is the bottom of the tree called?
Answer—The hem.

*　　*　　*

We were discussing seagulls.

Jamie—When it flies over the bay, it's called a *bagel*. (I thought that was quite clever.)

*　　*　　*

The speech teacher had been going over the *th* sound and asked the children to draw a picture of something that had that sound.

Some drew thread, thimbles, etc.

She asked James about his picture. He said, "This is a picture of a boy throwing up."

*　　*　　*

It was pouring rain, and Michael said, "It's a good thing I brought my umbrella, or I'd get soaking dry."

*   *   *

On the first snowfall of the year, Michael said, "Wow, I'm going outside and sled my sled."

*   *   *

We were paper weaving during activity time. Carol Ann had stopped working, so I asked her if she wished to continue the weaving.

She said, "No, not too quite."

*   *   *

Andrea brought a slinky to school and said it would go down 2, 3, or 4 steps, but wasn't sure how many.

She said, "I guess it can go down any much stairs."

*   *   *

Scott—This is my new um—.
This is my new um—.
It's new!

*   *   *

The custodian was using a squeegee on the outside of our classroom windows.

One of the children said, "Oh, look. He's shaving the windows!"

*   *   *

Emery—I'm straightening the toy because some-body turned it upside right.

*   *   *

3
Evasion

I had been absent from school for one day.

Tommy brought a little toy car for Show & Tell and said he found it on the way to school.

I said, "Perhaps it belongs to some other little boy who lost it."

He said, "No, the boy gave it to me."

I said, "Then the boy didn't lose it," and then questioned him a little further. By this time, he was fed up with my inquisitiveness and said, all in one breath, "Oh, I guess he lost it but he wanted another five-year-old-boy to have it, and Mrs. Kearns, I missed you when you weren't in school on Friday."

*   *   *

We had been cutting out a number 8 with 8 circles for number concept. Faith had pasted 11 circles. I said after we had counted them, "How many do you have to take off?" She said, "Some!"

*   *   *

We had a slight shortage of paper, so the rule was only 1 piece of "play" paper a day for each child.

J.K. to Jonathan, who had taken a 2nd piece—How many pieces of paper did you have today?

Jon—I only had one first.

*   *   *

One child had brought cupcakes to school to celebrate his birthday. They were set aside for snack time near the end of the day. During the early afternoon, we were doing a science lesson and we were deeply involved in a discussion about thermometers. One child was wildly waving his arm in the air, hoping, I thought, to impart some information about the subject under discussion. I said, "Yes, Joe?" Said he, "I don't like cupcakes!"

*   *   *

We were doing a number concept book and had reached #6. The children were to cut out a 6 and 6 circles. Susan had just 5 circles. I said, "Count." She did and I said, "You have only 5." She said, "Well, I counted fast."

*　　*　　*

Emery had his boots on backwards and I brought it to his attention.

Said he, "My *sister* changed them around this morning at home."

Ned—I have a book about when Bambi was a thawn.

J.K.—Fawn.

Ned—Thawn.

J.K.—Ned, put your upper teeth against your lower lip and say the word.

Ned—Thawn.

J.K.—Try again.

Ned—I have a book about when Bambi was a baby.

*　　*　　*

4
Pathos and/or Innocence

J.K.—"Michael, if you don't behave, you'll have to stay after school."

M.—"I can't (in tears). I haven't got my pajamas."

* * *

Randi—Mrs. K., have you any children?
J.K.—Yes, I have one son.
Randi—Only one?
J.K.—Yes.
Randi—(chuckling) Oh, you poor thing!

* * *

I had a child who was not too bright—not retarded, but somewhat slow.

I wrote his name on a piece of paper and told him to copy it 2 times.

As expected, he brought the paper back to me with it written only once.

I said, "Robert, how many times did I tell you to write your name?"

He said, "Two times."

I said, "All right, go back and write it 2 times."

He brought me the paper with a big *2* on it.

*   *   *

Jimmy—May I sit next to Jo-Jo if I promise not to talk?

J.K.—Yes. (Jimmy talks during lesson time—as expected and as usual.)

J.K.—Jimmy, what were you doing just now that you shouldn't have been doing?

Jimmy—Talking.

J.K.—I'll have to move you away from Jo-Jo. You broke your promise.

Jimmy—I know, but my promise is coming back!

*   *   *

J.K.—Michael, why are you so worried about staying after school?

Michael—(rubbing his eyes)—I can't see so good when it's dark.

*   *   *

Reported to me by Stacy's mother.

Stacy started out one A.M., turned back, went in the house, and said to his mother, "Mommy, we forgot to pray for me to be a good boy today."

*   *   *

We were making #4 and four circles for our number booklet. I stressed that the four must face in the right direction. I went around to each child to see if everyone had it correct, then told them to go ahead and paste. When I got to Bill, he said, "I know my 4 is right, but what I want to know is—are my balls on right?"

* * *

The school secretary and I had the same kind of shoes:

Adrienne—Mrs. Kearns, do you see those shoes Mrs. Lynch has on?

J.K.—Yes.

A.—Well, do you have the same kind?

J.K.—Yes.

A.—You never wear them on the same day she wears them, so I thought you were sharing them.

* * *

We were discussing "love" among family members:
1. "When my mother dies, I want to die right on top of her"—Amy.
2. "My mother *thinks* she likes me"—Anne.
3. Another child—"I'm sure my mommy loves me, but she's not sure I love her."

* * *

Dean—My mother ran over the cat and he died.

J.K.—Oh, I'm so very sorry.

Dean—It wasn't your fault. It was the cat's fault.

*   *   *

When I was writing on the blackboard, my chalk "squeaked" just a bit. Said one of the little girls, "Mrs. K., when you write on the board, I get cold." (I know the feeling!)

*   *   *

Ellen—When you stand on your head, all the water you drink goes in your head.

McCall—Does it feel good?

Ellen—Ick. No, it's awful.

*   *   *

Kate—We have a mommy hamster and we got a daddy for a few days. Today is the last day we'll have the daddy. Maybe the mommy will be pregnant tomorrow.

*   *   *

Bobby—A boy was hit by a bike and floated right up to the sky.

*   *   *

Our crossing guard died and the school had a tree planting in his memory.

Laurie—Is Uncle Tom an angel now?

J.K.—I guess he is.

L.—But I don't think he knows how to fly.

*   *   *

Chris—My mother came home from the hospital.

J.K.—I'm glad, but I didn't know she had been sick.

Chris—She wasn't sick. She just had some parts taken out.

*   *   *

Alan, during Show & Tell time:

I couldn't find my daddy. I looked all over for him. I went outside, then I went to the kitchen and the playroom and all over. Then I went to the bedroom, and Mrs. Kearns, do you know where I found him?

J.K.—No.

Alan—Under my mommy.

*   *   *

Little Robby always came to school looking like he just stepped out of a sand box.

Our classroom had a private bathroom just for the Kindergarten children, and one day, as I was sitting at my desk, Robby came out of the bathroom, walked right past the other children, holding up his slacks and underpants just below his buttocks, came up to me and said, "Mrs. Kearns, will you clean me?"

I said, "No, Robby, but let's go back to the bathroom, and I'll show you what to do."

We did that, and in a few minutes, after I had gone back to my desk, out came Robby again, with the clothes in the same location (under the buttocks). He stood beside me, bent over so I could see his little rear, and said, "Am I clean?"

*   *   *

5
Reporters

Kelly had a stye in one eye.

J.K.—Is your mother doing anything about that stye, Kelly?

Kelly—Yes, she's hoping it will go away.

* * *

Jane—"Daddy was mad at Mommy, so he pushed her food over."

J.K.—"What did Mommy do?"

Jane—"Then *she* got mad."

* * *

Mark had just hit a little girl.

I said to him, "Mark, that isn't nice. We don't hit little girls. Your father doesn't hit your mother."

Said Mark, "Oh, yes, he does—when he's mad at her!"

* * *

We were discussing doctors and what they do for us. The children were naming their own Dr., and Dr. R's name was mentioned several times. Ricky spoke up and said, "We used to have Dr. R, but he was horsin' around with my mother—now we have Dr. T."

*　　*　　*

Bobby—When my mother came home from the hospital with my baby sister, our sitter said to her, "You ought to get up and do some work."

J.K.—That wasn't a very nice thing for her to say to your mother.

Bobby—It certainly wasn't nice. She doesn't know what life is like—and—my mother got a new sitter!

*　　*　　*

Michael brought a pilot's hat for Show & Tell.
I said, "Did you get that when you were on a trip?"
"No," said Mike, "*one* of my daddies brought it."

*　　*　　*

50

Mary had been dreaming a great deal and reported the dreams to her mother. One morning when she awakened, she couldn't remember the dreams. She said to her mother, "I didn't dream last night. All the programs were turned off."

*   *   *

Patrick—We're moving to Cleveland to a big white house that's clean!

*   *   *

Dean asked me to button the waistband of his pants, as they were a little difficult for him to handle. I teased him by saying, "You have a big tummy!"

He said, "That's nothing. My mommy has a bigger one!" (She was *very* pregnant.)

*   *   *

Adrienne—Mrs. Kearns, when you had a husband, did you have one bed for both of you?

J.K.—Yes, I did.

Adrienne—My mother and daddy have two beds.

*   *   *

Ken—I get nervous when I try to make my *2*s.

J.K.—No need to get nervous. Take your time and you'll learn.

Ken—My father gets nervous when he has to turn the car fast. He says, "God dammit."

*   *   *

6
Just for Fun

I had read a book about the Pilgrims that told that they went to Holland before coming to America.

In review, the next day, I asked the children where the Pilgrims went after leaving England.

Said one little girl, "Brooklyn."

*   *   *

I asked George if the new baby in the family was a boy or girl.

Said he, "A boy."

Piped up another child (happy that his was the same), "My baby brother is a boy, too."

*   *   *

J.K.—Matthew, that's a nice shirt you're wearing.
Matt—I know.
J.K.—Is it new?
Matt—Is what new?

*   *   *

The children used the expression, "I have to make," when they wished to go to the bathroom. Because I objected to this expression, I said to one little girl who had just said it, "You mean you have to go to the bathroom. You don't *make* anything when you go in there."

Pulling herself up to her full height, she said, "Oh, *yes, I do!*"

*   *   *

David, entering the room for the P.M. session, said all in one breath—"Good afternoon, may I go get a toy now?"

*   *   *

Christine, age 5, brought in two stuffed animals. "This one," she said, "I had when I was a baby. The other one I had when I was a child."

*   *   *

Why weren't you in school yesterday, Keith?
Keith—My mother couldn't cart her star.

*   *   *

Eddie—Mrs. Kearns, are you a grandmother?
J.K.—No, Eddie, I'm not (I was 45). Why, do I look like one?
Eddie—Yes, you look a little old!

*   *   *

I'm sure the next statement was not original, but something Erin heard and remembered. "All the animals in Noah's ark came in pairs except the worms. They came in apples."

*   *   *

Patrick—We're going to have a new room built, and I'm going to move into it.

J.K.—What are you going to do with your old room?

Patrick—Oh, just throw it into the garbage.

*   *   *

One of the little girls showed a picture of a 1913 auto. I said, "That was made before I was born." (I was 46 at the time.) "Oh," she said. "Then it must *really* be old."

*   *   *

Christine (bringing a friend to school).—Hello, Mrs. Kearns. This little girl is Vicky.

J.K.—Hello, Vicky.

Chris to Vicky—How did she know you?

*   *   *

1st Boy—You can't play with my blocks unless you ask me.

2nd Boy—Can I play with your blocks?

1st Boy—No.

*   *   *

Karen—"Mrs. Kearns, me and Michael are going to marry each other. I just have to get his phone number first."

*   *   *

My mother couldn't find her key cars.

*   *   *

Eileen—My mother is in the hospital.
J.K.—That's too bad. What is the matter with her?
Eileen—She went to get a scar.

*   *   *

Angela (a model)—My mother and I have to go to N.Y. today to see the man I used to work for.
J.K.—Perhaps he has another job for you.
Angela—I don't know, but one more commercial, and I'll be in Hollywood!

*   *   *

Thomas—I ate too fast and it made me feel like I was crying on the inside and laughing on the outside.

*   *   *

Robert—I had a tummy ache, but I feel better now because I pushed it out.

*   *   *

Complaint department!
Eddie—The people at my table said I can't be Jewish and Catholic and American!

*   *   *

7
Just Statements

Linda—Mrs. Kearns, I bet you're wondering how my mother is feeling.

J.K.—Well, Linda, how *is* she feeling?

Linda—Why, she's just fine!

*   *   *

Thursday was the day for presenting our annual operetta. Pat asked, on Tuesday, if his younger brother could come along with his mother.

I said, "Yes, if he can be nice and quiet so everyone can hear the songs."

Pat said, "He can practice being quiet tomorrow!"

*   *   *

We were discussing the last space shot and Richard said, "The pictures on TV were dumb, but when you're small, you don't understand things like that."

*   *   *

Anne—"I'm going to marry my daddy when I grow up."

J.K.—But he's already married.

Anne—That's all right. He can get married again.

J.K.—But what about your mother?

Anne—Oh, someone else can marry her!

*　　*　　*

J.K.—"Why do we have Flag Day?"

Child—"Because the pool is opening next week."

*　　*　　*

Santa is bringing me a sled after Christmas. He tripped on the stairs and stepped on the one he was supposed to bring on Christmas Eve.

*　　*　　*

It was May and Rachel asked if she could sing a Thanksgiving song she remembered.

One child asked, "How come you still know that?"

Rachel, "I'm pretty smart, you know."

*　　*　　*

During Show & Tell time, Joe was showing a toy limousine.

J.K.—Tell us what this is.

Joe—This is mine.

*　　*　　*

We were discussing time and had reached six, half past six or 30 minutes after six.

Jaime (age 6 ½)—"I'm six-thirty."

*　　*　　*

Question by me—"How many children plan to hang their stockings for Christmas?"

Jewish youngster—"I can't. I've got my stockings on!"

* * *

One little five-year old was looking at the manuscript work done by another five-year old, and asked, "Whose work is that?"

I said, "This was done by Jay."

Said the youngster, "That's very good for his age."

* * *

Alan—My aunt has a girl dog and her name is Co-quette.

J.K.—Is she a French poodle?

Alan—No, she's a Jewish dog.

* * *

AND
from whence cometh the title
Eddie—My grandmother has a chandelier.
Doug—That's NOTHING. My daddy has a Chevy.

*   *   *

8
Other Stories

Each year in the late spring, parents of the children entering school the following fall were invited to a meeting with the Kindergarten teachers.

We advised the parents about many things that would put the youngsters at ease.

One very important point to stress was the fact that, if the child was always called by a nickname, it was most vital that he or she be told his "real" first name.

One particular year stands out in my memory.

On the first day of school, if the weather was good, I would stand outside my Kindergarten room, calling out the names of the children who would enter my classroom.

Many times there were pre-school brothers and sisters observing.

I called the first four or five names and reached a *Margaret Smith.* I repeated the name two or three times, got no reply, and finishing the list, repeated Margaret's full names. No answer.

Finally, up piped a little voice from the sidelines, and pointing to a child standing close, said, "That girl's mother's name is *Mrs.* Smith."

I asked the child her name, and, of course, she said, "Peggy."

Obviously, the youngster had never been called any name but "Peggy," and had no knowledge of her given name.

In line with this item, I received the following note and short story from one of the parents, and I'd like to share them with you.

Dear Mrs. Kearns,

I couldn't resist sending you this short story. Seems to me I remember some sage advice you delivered at a kindergarten tea 2 years ago about this very thing. The author must have overheard you and turned it into a charming story, which I hope will give you a chuckle.

C.E.

Roll Call
by Katinka Loeser

On the first day of school—and it was a beautiful September day—Miss Betty Martin, young, slim, friendly, stood smiling by the door of the kindergarten room as the children settled into their chairs after the morning recess. It was Betsy's first day at school too, her very first as a teacher. She adored children this age, four and five—shy little girls in bright, brief dresses; self-conscious little boys in shorts and slacks. She sat down in her own chair; on her left was a jumble of enrichment materials, on her right a tank of tropical fish.

"Now, boys and girls, because this our first day, I'm going to take attendance again," she explained. "And as you learned this morning, that is when I say your name and you answer, 'Here.' "

"Here," a few children said.

"That is right," Betsy said. "But too soon. Only when I say your name. This is the way a teacher finds out who is in school and who is not in school, isn't it?"

The class nodded soberly.

"Just in case someone has to stay home with the sniffles one day," she went on, closing one eye knowingly. Then, looking down at her attendance sheet, she said, "Thomas Anderson."

"Me," Thomas Anderson said, staring haughtily at his peers.

"Thomas Anderson is here," Betsy said. "Lynn Arcudi."

"Here," Lynn Arcudi said loudly, and then clapped her right hand over her mouth.

Almost through the *D*s, Betsy said, "William Dinsmore." There was no answer. Betsy looked closely at the attendance sheet. She couldn't have made a mistake; he had been there before recess—there was a check by his name. "William Dinsmore," she said again, but nobody said anything. "Will William Dinsmore please say 'here'?" Betsy said.

But he didn't.

"Now, who among us is a friend of William Dinsmore's?" Betsy asked the class.

There was no response from the group; they simply sat there, waiting for the next question.

"Who played with William at recess?" she asked. "Think hard." She screwed up her forehead and so did the children.

Betsy finished the attendance report; the paper was

not as steady in her hand as it had been a few minutes before. She picked some names. "Let me see. John Mercier may go to the cupboard and get the crayons and Ralph Miller may pass them out. Susan Slater may get the paper and Elizabeth Gantz may pass it out. Everyone else may get ready to color."

As the children got busy, Betsy walked over to the wall telephone and buzzed the office. Mr. Jackson's secretary, Mrs. Prince, said, "Yes, Betsy?"

"I have a problem," Betsy said. "I wonder if someone could take over here for a moment."

Mrs. Prince hesitated. "Well, Hester Schlegel has a free period now. I'll send her right in."

When Hester Schlegel came in Betsy addressed the class. "Now, children, Mrs. Schlegel is going to be in the room while you color, and I'll be right back. And William Dinsmore is going to say 'here' before I leave, isn't he?"

He did not.

In the office Betsy explained to Mrs. Prince, who immediately called Mr. Jackson, a calm, thin man.

"He's got to be here," Mr. Jackson said when he heard the story. "Let's not get excited. Are you sure of your attendance sheet?"

"Definitely," Betsy Martin said.

"What does he look like?" Mr. Jackson asked.

"Look like?" Betsy said. "I don't know. There are twenty-six children in that room whom I've never seen until this morning."

Mr. Jackson said, "Yes, of course. Well, let's go take a look around the playground. Maybe he's hiding in the barrel game."

"Don't forget the pond," Mrs. Prince said.

"What pond?" Betsy asked.

"The pond the Community Garden Club gave us last year," Mrs. Prince said. "With water lilies. It was their landscaping project."

There was no one on the playground, in the barrels, or in the pond. Mr. Jackson and Betsy went back into the building.

"Call the boy's mother," Mr. Jackson told Mrs. Prince. "And now," he went on, "we must explore all of the possibilities. He may have gone home. Maybe he just didn't like it here."

Mrs. Prince said, "Nobody home there."

"Very well, now, if he started home," Mr. Jackson said, "he—by the way, where does he live? What bus?"

They looked up the schedules and the Dinsmore address.

"Dear me," the principal said with interest, "there are many roads he could have taken home. He could even have taken Main Street."

Betsy's chin quivered.

"If he took Main Street," Mr. Jackson said, "that is a highway, and therefore under the jurisdiction of the state police. Mrs. Prince, get me the barracks, please."

Mrs. Prince looked at her list of emergency numbers and called one. "They're sending a car immediately," she reported. "They want to know what he looks like and how he is dressed."

"Tell them we don't know," Mr. Jackson said. "And keep trying the Dinsmore house."

"What about the town police?" Mrs. Prince asked.

"Of course," Mr. Jackson said.

Mrs. Prince telephoned. "Captain Massiello is ordering cars to cover all the side roads radiating from the school," she reported.

"Now," Mr. Jackson said, "tell the custodians to check the building." He rubbed his jaw. "We must keep cool and try to think," he said as four massive state troopers tramped in.

"Did you look on both sides of the road?" he asked.

They nodded.

The two custodians came in, shaking their heads. There was the sound of sirens on the side roads.

"Mrs. Dinsmore doesn't answer." Mrs. Prince said.

"She must have a reference," the principal said.

Mrs. Prince looked in her file. "Of course; here it is. 'In case parent cannot be reached, call BR nine-nine-one-eight-nine.' " Everybody watched her closely as she began to speak. "Oh, Mrs. Dinsmore is there, having coffee?" she said. "Yes, of course, I understand what a relief it is to have the children out of the house and in school. May I speak to her, please?" She did, briefly, and looked up. "She'll be right over."

They all cleared their throats and waited until a tall woman in wrinkled Madras shorts with matching blouse, her hair in pink foam-rubber curlers, ran in the front door and down the hall, followed by two town policemen.

"We clocked this woman going fifty in a twenty-five-mile zone," one of the policemen said.

"Just a minute," Mr. Jackson said.

"My Lord," Mrs. Dinsmore said. "What has happened?"

Mr. Jackson seated her on a chair. "Nothing to be alarmed about," he said. "But we think your son may have wandered off. We want a complete description. Please try to keep calm, Mrs. Dinsmore, and help us."

Mrs. Dinsmore clutched her curlers. "He's five years old," she said, "and he's got blue eyes and blond hair and a crew cut." She swallowed hard. "He wore new tan chinos and a red-and-white striped T-shirt and new white sneakers."

"Any identifying scars or anything like that?" a state trooper asked.

Mrs. Dinsmore put both hands over her mouth and stared at him.

"Now, just a minute, Lieutenant," Mr. Jackson said. "Before we go on, I want to take the boy's mother into the kindergarten room. She may see a child she knows who can help us in some way."

They all went to the kindergarten room, opened the door, and went in. Mrs. Dinsmore glanced rapidly along the tables where the children were busy, and then she stopped abruptly, raised her hands in front of her, and cried, "Why, there he is!" She pointed.

The stalwart state troopers stood by the table of enrichment materials. The town policemen put their hands on their hips; the two custodians looked at each other and yawned. Betsy Martin, Mr. Jackson, and Mrs. Prince followed the direction of Mrs. Dinsmore's finger. Mrs. Dinsmore advanced into the room.

"What are you doing here?" she demanded.

The boy with the crew cut and the new sneakers said, "Coloring."

Mrs. Dinsmore took more steps into the room. "Why didn't you answer when the teacher called your name?" she said.

"She didn't say my name," the boy answered, continuing to color.

And then Betsy Martin went forward. "Why, yes, I did, dear," she said. "Don't you remember when I took attendance?"

The boy looked at his mother.

"She didn't say my name. She said William Dinsmore. My name's Bill." And then Bill Dinsmore burst into tears, holding his red crayon stiffly before him. THE END.

A fitting story found in another publication.

Show and Tell
Teachers Don't Have All The Luck;
Sometimes They Have Children Like Mine
by Marie Scholding

When my daughter Barbara grows up, she will be adored by the PTA because she is the world's number one volunteer. She has volunteered (my services, of course) for everything from baking cupcakes to a home away from home for five tadpoles and three sweet potatoes. She has also volunteered the state of our family finances, and the new word she learned when Daddy dropped a can of apple juice on his toe.

These revelations generally occur during sessions of Show and Tell, when the children bring in interesting objects to show the class—but I honestly don't believe the teacher meant things like the overdue electric bill my son Chris took in.

"Are you sure Miss Trainer wants you to bring these things to school?" I asked him one day as he headed for the school bus with a dead snake.

"You can take anything to school but a horse," he said, "because you can't get a horse on the bus." Which is logical.

Barbara is carrying on the tradition. But I doubt that even her teacher was as surprised as her grandmother was, when she took her grandmother's false teeth. She took very good care of them, however, having packed them in straw along with her pet mouse.

Insects, dead or alive, are always favorites with children if not with the teacher. Barbara's class had a substitute teacher for three days after she took a praying mantis cocoon that hatched.

Miss Trainer must be an angel of patience to pretend interest in such items as a dirty balloon, half a hot dog, a broken comb, a bird skeleton, and a collection of paper napkins saved from birthday parties, not to mention a parking ticket and an "I Like Ike" button.

Luckily, I caught Barbara before she reached school with her baby brother, but I wasn't so fortunate with my old diary and the neighbor's "For Sale" sign.

Show and Tell is no longer part of the curriculum in our school. I can understand why.

9
My Family

In explanation of family names:
Jack—My nickname for son John
Johnny—Grandson John
Jackie—Granddaughter Jacqueline

*   *   *

When Johnny was four my son took him into a restaurant's men's room, went into the cubicle to see that he was situated correctly, then waited for him outside the cubicle. There was another man present, washing his hands. When Johnny came out to the sink area, he said to his dad, "You are the best daddy in the whole world." The stranger laughed gently, causing Johnny to say, "Don't laugh. It's just an expression!"

*   *   *

Jack was born when my late husband and I lived in Miami, Florida, in the forties. He (Jack) has reminded his children, on occasion, about his birth city and said he would show them Miami someday.

That someday arrived when the children were two and three—(granddaughter—2 and grandson—3).

There was a medical conference in Fort Lauderdale and the decision was made to take the entire family.

The day after they arrived, Kathy, my daughter-in-law, said to the children, "We're going to show you Miami tomorrow." Johnny said, "I don't want to see your ami, I want to see Daddy's ami."

*　　*　　*

Said Jackie, age four, after being scolded, "That's humiliating!"

*   *   *

I visited my family and stayed just overnight. It was May and Jackie said, "I wish you could stay longer—every night in May," but, after a moment's hesitation, said—"Guess I'd get sick of you then!"

*   *   *

A conversation with my grandson:
Me—You're nice, Johnny.
Johnny—Sometimes I push Jackie and that's not nice.
Me—True. Some of the things you do are not nice, but you're still nice.
Johnny—I'm nice to you.
Me—Yes. All the time.
Johnny—Oh, that's nice of me.

*   *   *

Johnny at age five, couldn't make a decision about what he wanted after being told he could have *1* toy. He hemmed and hawed and made a small scene after changing his mind a few times.

Later, after finally making a decision, his parents told him he would have to stop that nonsense or he would get nothing.

He thought about that a minute and said, "That sounds like a threat!"

*   *   *

My son had joined the cross-country team in his school.

Being just a fair runner, he said that during practice, when they ran around the lake, the other students were so far ahead of him, he couldn't see them around the bend.

I offered what I thought was the proper amount of sympathy and understanding.

He said, "Oh, I don't mind. It makes me feel as if I'm first."

*   *   *

Johnny, age six, was playing with a toy "from Santa." (He still believed.) He proceeded to tell his dad the story of Santa's workshop in the North Pole and the follow-up of toys to the children.

Being an early reader, he said to his dad, "If the toys are made in the North Pole, why does it say, 'Made in Italy?' "

My son's answer—"It must be made in the Italian part of the North Pole!"

*　　*　　*

Jackie, age five, had called me on the phone. We talked awhile and finished our chat. A few minutes later, my phone rang again and it was Jackie saying she had forgotten to tell me something. She said, "I'm sorry the phone had to ring again."

I said, "I don't mind if I can talk to you."

She said, "I think I'm losing my voice."

I said, "Do you have a cold?"

"No," she answered, "I just talk a lot."

*　　*　　*

At holiday time I have always sent my grandchildren a card containing a dollar or two (as I'm sure all grandparents do).

When I was preparing to visit China, I said to Johnny, age four, "I'll send you a card from China."

His answer: "Will there be a dollar in it?"

*   *   *

Johnny, age five, and his dad were watching a cartoon showing a wolf chasing a chicken into a coop. The wolf got a poker to try to push the chicken out. Jack said, "He's fishing for the chicken." Johnny said, "He's not fishing. He's chickening." (My literal-minded grandson.)

*   *   *

I had a pencil holder that had been given to me by a Kindergarten child. Johnny admired it, and I said he could have it.

He thought it over and said, "I feel badly about taking this away from you, but I guess I'd feel worse if I didn't take it."

*   *   *

Jack was telling me about a discussion he and Johnny, six, had one night when he (Johnny) was being tucked in at bedtime.

Johnny—Where do babies come from?

Jack—From the mother's womb.

Johnny—I know that, but how does it get there?

Jack—Seeds from the Mother and Father.

Johnny—How do the seeds get there?

Jack, to me—I said what every good, red-blooded American father says—"Johnny, it's late. Go to sleep."

*   *   *

Jack (my son at age fifteen) was told to write a 500-word composition (for punishment) about aviation, one of his interests.

He drew a picture of a plane, tore it in half, and handed in one-half with this note:

"Brother Alfred—If a picture is worth a thousand words, this ought to be good for five hundred."

(Fortunately, Brother Alfred had a good sense of humor!)

*   *   *

Epilogue

To the children:

My time with you over the years was a bright light in my life, and I hope the readers have felt the warmth of that light.

To the teachers and other staff members with whom I was associated all those years:

We shared a few tears and many, many laughs, and I thank you for that.